Original title:
Ripples Beneath the Tide

Copyright © 2025 Creative Arts Management OÜ
All rights reserved.

Author: Evelyn Hartman
ISBN HARDBACK: 978-1-80587-378-5
ISBN PAPERBACK: 978-1-80587-848-3

Waves of Introspection

In the ocean's deep, thoughts swirl and dive,
Like fish that dance, they kick and jive.
I ponder life while skimming stones,
A sea of laughter, and silly tones.

Seagulls caw, they steal my fries,
While I muse on clouds that lie in disguise.
Each splash a secret, each wave a jest,
Who knew the sea was such a quest?

Footprints in sand, a sketch of the day,
I trace my worries, then watch them stray.
The ebb and flow, a playful tease,
As laughter drips like honey from trees.

With every tide, I giggle and grin,
The ocean's a mirror where silliness begins.
I surf on absurdity, hang ten on wit,
In this watery realm where silliness sits.

The Secrets That Linger

Between the waves, fish whisper low,
Tales of sailors and where they go.
Secrets floating like corks on high,
As I laugh at clouds that sail pass by.

A crab in a tux, he's quite the sight,
Dancing with seaweed in moonlit night.
Shells gossip loudly, oh what a scene,
With tales of treasure that can't be seen.

Starfish share chuckles, oh such delight,
As they tumble and twist in the cool moonlight.
Bubbles blow kisses, as they rise and pop,
While octopuses juggle, they never stop.

The ocean's a stage, with all its quirks,
Where laughter and silliness go berserk.
So when you dive deep, just keep your mind free,
For this aquatic party is full of glee!

The Temptation of Stillness

In a pond where frogs conspire,
Laziness may start to tire.
Suddenly a splash, so grand,
That frog leaps far, and he's unplanned!

Stillness calls like a cozy chair,
But the splash was quite the scare.
"Oh no!" croaked the frog in fright,
Was it a fish, or just a kite?

Currents of the Soul

Bubbles rise with a chuckle loud,
Exploring depths where secrets crowd.
"Is that a fish or just my shoe?"
It turns out, it's someone's canoe!

The water swirls, and laughter spreads,
While seaweed waves like dance floors tread.
"Oh dear!" yells a crab with flair,
"I swear these currents just don't care!"

Diverging Paths

Two fish meet at a fork in flow,
One says left, while right's aglow.
"I'll take the chance for a tasty bait!"
But misses dinner—what a fate!

The other giggles, swims away,
"Perhaps I'll find a better way!"
Suddenly, a turtle shows up,
And says, "Did you forget your cup?"

Beneath the Calm Surface

Underneath, the party's on,
Neon colors, fish have drawn!
"Yo fishy friend, let's break the mold!"
"Dance with me; don't be too bold!"

The surface shimmers, all looks fine,
Yet down below, there's wine and vine.
A clam croons tunes from way back when,
Saying "Let's jam 'til daylight then!"

Serenade of the Submerged

Bubbles rise with tales to share,
Fish in hats float without a care.
A crab sings songs of ocean pride,
While octopuses dance, all they hide.

Seahorses giggle in their parade,
Wand'ring through the kelp they invaded.
Jellyfish juggle, what a sight,
In underwater disco, day turns to night.

The Sway of Silent Waters

The turtles plod with swagger bold,
In shades of green and flecks of gold.
They tell the fish just how to groove,
While seaweed sways, it's quite the move.

Starfish laugh, they cannot climb,
They twirl in circles, not in line.
A dolphin's joke, we must all hear,
Echoes beneath, but oh so near.

Beneath the Cresting Waves

A clam's in line for fancy shoes,
While eels tell tales of deep-sea blues.
They twirl and swirl in water's spree,
Where sharks chase dreams while sipping tea.

Corals argue who's the brightest,
Anemones bob with glee and slightness.
In the surf, the guppies zoom,
While the grouper drums a funky tune.

Whispers in the Endless Blue

The pelicans dive with style so grand,
While fish compete in a winged band.
Snails tell jokes about their speed,
While dolphins dance, oh what a breed!

A whale hums softly, "What's the fuss?"
As krill organize a little bus.
In the frothy sea, laughter flows,
As the ocean's secret, everybody knows.

Distant Calls from Below

Bubbles whisper secrets to fish,
Swimming past, they giggle and swish.
A crab tells tales of floating shoes,
While seahorses laugh at bad news.

Starfish dance like they own the floor,
Singing to shells, they always want more.
The seaweed sways in a frolicsome spree,
As dolphins share jokes, just like you and me.

Heartbeats in the Waves

Waves hum a tune of joyful cheer,
As clams chuckle, trying to hear.
The otters slide down the big blue hill,
While jellyfish jiggle, quite the thrill.

Each splash from a fish sounds like laughter,
Their flops and splashes create great banter.
The seagulls squawk, joining the fun,
Making a ruckus in the warm sun.

Ocean's Secrets Unsaid

The octopus paints with colors bright,
Creating art in the soft moonlight.
While fishes gossip about their day,
Shells hide secrets in a mischievous way.

Beneath the waves, they hoot and laugh,
Planning parties for the next big gaffe.
Barnacles cling on with a sly grin,
Whispering plans, hoping to win.

Beneath the Murky Waters

In the murk, the catfish play hide and seek,
While turtles chuckle, so cool and sleek.
The rumors spread of a sunken shoe,
What adventures might that old leather do?

Prawns tap dance on the silt below,
As frogs croak along in a show.
Another laugh comes from a rogue eel,
Tickling the depths with an electric feel.

Ghosts of the Deep Blue

In the ocean's shimmery glow,
Ghosts dance to a tune, you know.
They bubble and giggle with glee,
Scaring fish as they survey the sea.

Watch out for their ticklish rays,
Messing up your beachy days!
They sneak under boats with a splash,
Leaving sailors to squeak and dash.

A jellyfish jokes and plays around,
Floating like it owns the ground.
While octopuses snicker with delight,
Wrapped in a seaweed blanket at night.

Oh, those phantoms in azure hues,
Making mischief, it's what they choose!
With each wave that crashes and sways,
Underneath, they keep laughing always.

The Hidden Song of the Sea

Bubbles sing like oompah bands,
With dolphins clapping in the sands.
A fortune cookie held in a clam,
Might just tell you a joke or spam.

Seashells whisper silly rhymes,
Making waves do funny climbs.
A starfish with a silly face,
Cracks up crabs in a merry race.

Tidal tunes play peekaboo,
With shrimps that dance like a conga crew.
Surfboards giggle as they ride the swell,
Carrying stories that no one can tell.

Beneath the foam, laughter grows,
Where sea cucumbers strike poses, who knows?
In every splash, a jest awaits,
The hidden song that bubbles and creates.

Glimmers of Truth in Turbulence

In the frothy waves, truths collide,
Seagulls squawk, take it all in stride.
The crabs complain while shells are tossed,
Lamenting their luck—and what it cost.

Surfers tumble, they laugh in falls,
Waves that greet them with splashing calls.
The truth is out, it seems so clear,
Water's got jokes and a hearty cheer.

Beneath a wave, a fish spills tea,
About a whale who danced for glee.
Had a fin-finding good time today,
While shrimp played pranks and stole his tray.

Every swirl has a quip or two,
Amidst the chaos, giggles accrue.
In the sea's embrace, we find our muse,
Turbulence brings out the silly blues.

Waves of Change in Stillness

Amidst calm waters, a secret swirls,
Fish tell tales of their underwater pearls.
A turtle snickers as it glides by,
Dreaming of the day it'll fly in the sky.

Seashells gossip about the shore,
Sharing stories of what's in store!
A crab scuttles in and out of the reeds,
Planting a garden of funny seeds.

The calm waves wink and play peekaboo,
Like a friendly tide with a cheerful view.
A starfish plays hopscotch on the sand,
While seaweed dances, dreams unplanned.

Change is coming, but oh, what fun,
With waves that frolic under the sun.
In tranquil depths, humor expands,
As laughter ripples through ocean bands.

Interwoven Stories of the Sea

There once was a fish with a hat,
It danced on the waves, oh, imagine that!
With a flip and a flop, it spun in delight,
Drawing laughter from crabs in the warm sea light.

A turtle named Ted wore a shoe,
Claiming fashion was vital for him too.
He strutted the shore with a confident glide,
While seagulls giggled at his marine pride.

Threads of Connection

A clam and a shrimp shared a home,
They argued each day about sea foam.
'Tis mine!' said the clam, with a flash of his shell,
'But I'm the better swimmer,' the shrimp would yell.

Along came a octopus, quiet as night,
Offering peace with a wink and a slight.
'Let's knit a fine net, let's weave it with care,
And capture the jellyfish lingering there!'

Driftwood Dreams

A log floated by with a grin so wide,
Singing love songs to the nearby tide.
Fish swam in chorus, a splashing affair,
While dolphins rolled over, tossing their hair.

Then a catfish appeared, in a top hat and suit,
"A party!" he shouted, "Let's all salute!"
Grouchy old barnacles grumbled and sighed,
But even they chuckled; it's hard to divide!

The Narrative of the Sea

In a whirlpool of giggles, the tales would unfold,
Of mermaids who skateboarded—wonders untold.
With jellyfish as helmets and starfish for cheer,
They carved out the waves, spreading joy, oh dear!

A crab with a moustache cooked crumpets galore,
For all the sea critters who danced on the shore.
They feasted on laughter, with waves as their song,
In the heart of the ocean, where fun never's wrong.

Surging Stories from Below

In the depths where fish do dance,
A crab in shorts takes a silly chance.
With a flip and a flop, he declares a race,
But the seaweed pranks, oh, what a chase!

A dolphin laughs, turns a flip so quick,
While the octopus titters, feeling quite slick.
They play hide and seek in coral's embrace,
A comical chaos, oh, what a place!

The Quiet Power of the Ocean

Beneath the waves, a secret lair,
The turtles gossip without a care.
A seal in sunglasses lounges and sways,
Making sunbathers feel quite out of place!

A clam tells tales of deep-sea flight,
While starfish compete for the best tan light.
With laughter bubbling, the surf gets loud,
As the kraken joins in, feeling so proud!

Mysteries Among the Tides

Beneath the foam, a treasure lies,
A rubber ducky in a big sea guise.
The fish claim it's a relic of fame,
While a seagull squawks, "Oh, what a shame!"

Anemones giggle, waving like fans,
As barnacles plan their odd little pranks.
Who knew the depths could hold such cheer?
With jellyfish dancing, it's a comedy sphere!

Ripples of Time's Embrace

In the shallows, shells whisper tales,
Of sea foam parties and windy gales.
A lobster tries to master a dance,
While the tides just chuckle at his mischance!

Waves lapping softly, like a ticklish tease,
Mermaids with giggles sway in the breeze.
As the sun dips low, the fishes unite,
For a silly soiree under the moonlight!

Secrets of the Ocean Bed

In the depths where fish dance round,
A crab tried to wear a crown.
He pinched at clams with all his might,
But his throne was just a shell, polite!

A turtle surfed on a seaweed wave,
Claimed he was brave, oh how he'd rave!
But a jellyfish gave him a zap,
Now he's telling tales from a comfy lap.

Seahorses giggle with tiny gasps,
While dolphins tease with splashy clasps.
An octopus paints with ink so bright,
Creating murals that spark delight!

Goldfish gossip in a sunken wreck,
"Did you hear about the man in a tech?"
He tried to dive for treasure, oh what a sight,
He only found his shoelace that night!

The Drift of Distant Echoes

Out at sea where whispers twirl,
A clam claimed it was once a pearl.
It showed its friends with great delight,
But turned out it was just a bite!

The seaweed sang a silly song,
As starfish twirled, they thought they'd prong.
But when the tide came rolling in,
They tumbled over, what a spin!

A shark with dreams of being grand,
Joined a band, oh wasn't it planned?
But when he tried to play a tune,
The fish all laughed and fled by noon!

Bubble parties, fishy fun,
Seagulls cackling, "We've just begun!"
Under the waves, they pull a prank,
And laugh at sailors who lose their rank!

Whispers in the Water

In the shallows where secrets sprinkle,
Lobsters tell tales that make you crinkle.
With pinch of wit and a wink of eye,
They laugh at the fish that swam too high!

Fish in goggles swim in a line,
Chasing bubbles, oh how divine!
But when they splash, they cause a stir,
Making waves, oh what a blur!

An anemone sways with grace,
On a snail's back, oh, what a race!
But with one slip and a dizzy spin,
They laughed so hard they couldn't win!

Whales serenade with voices grand,
Sending echoes across the sand.
While octopuses hide with flair,
"Don't let them know, or we'll run bare!"

Underneath the Calm

Where the water whispers in soft embrace,
A clam decides to pick up pace.
He wanted a ride, a thrill or two,
But missed the boat, oh what a view!

A fish in a suit, quite the display,
Tried to dine in a fancy café.
But the waiter was a sneaky eel,
Who zapped his charm, oh what a deal!

Seahorses twirl in a waltz so grand,
While crabs do the cha-cha on the sand.
But when a wave gives a playful shove,
They tumble and giggle, full of love!

The ocean floor tells jokes so rare,
With seashells giggling in salty air.
Just remember, if you dive down low,
There's laughter waiting, this I know!

Echoes of the Present

In the water, fish make a scene,
Bubbles tickle the toes of a queen,
The crab wears a crown, quite absurd,
While seagulls plot gossip, quite overheard.

A dolphin jokes, surfacing high,
While octopuses wave a tentacled 'hi!',
They giggle and splash, no care in the world,
As a clam keeps the secrets, ever unfurled.

The Dance of the Unknown

In shadows below, something sways,
A fish in a tutu, dancing always,
Seaweed joins in, a glittering twist,
As the starfish says, 'You're too good to miss!'

A jellyfish bobbles, a flouncy parade,
While the seashells gossip in shade and charade,
Who knew the ocean could throw such a ball?
It's a wild water party and you're invited to call!

Tides of Uncertainty

The waves waddle in, like they're late for a date,
Shells hold their breath, the outcome's a weight,
A turtle rolls in, all covered in glee,
While a flatfish sighs, 'This isn't for me.'

The currents can't decide, they toss and they throw,
Sandy surprises set one in a flow,
The clowns of the sea, with antics so sly,
Remind us that chaos can also mean 'why?'

The Beneath and Beyond

What's lurking down there? A treasure or fright?
An eel with a top hat, quite ready to bite,
With laughter he wiggles, 'No fear, I'm a friend!'
Join in on the mischief, let madness transcend!

A rock with a grudge sings a grumpy old tune,
While hermit crabs dance under the moon,
The depths hold their quirks, their charm without end,
Making waves of joy with a wink and a bend.

Waves of Heartfelt Emotion

A splash of laughter in the sea,
Where jellyfish dance so merrily.
Seagulls pluck fries from beach-goers,
And waves chuckle as they roar, sir.

Flip-flops fly, socks lost at play,
Sandcastle kings, they rule the day.
Each wave a joke, each tide a prank,
The ocean's humor, can't be blank.

Bubbles blowing by like dreams,
Fish grinning wide with silly schemes.
Confetti of foam, a playful fight,
Oh, under the sun, everything feels right.

So let's ride the surf with a grin,
Dive into the fun, let's begin.
Weather's fine for a giggling plunge,
In this sea of joy, there's always a lunge.

The Hidden Voyage

A ship of dreams sets sail afresh,
With ducks as crew and barge to mesh.
Oar strokes wave with a clumsy cheer,
Lazy fish wave back, 'Oh, dear!'

Around each bend, a surprise we find,
Giggling crabs with treasure twined.
Octopuses juggling shells so bright,
It's a carnival under the moonlight.

The map is lost, just like my mind,
Chasing waves, so unrefined.
But who needs charts, when laughter's key,
To navigate this fun-filled spree.

The currents pull, but I do not care,
This silly quest is all that's fair.
So hoist the flag, let's roam and roam,
In a wacky ocean, we've found our home.

Tides of Transformation

A hermit crab in a fancy shell,
Struts on the sand, 'Oh, isn't he swell?'
With a twirl and a wave, he shows his style,
While starfish chuckle, they're in for a while.

The beach is a stage, the crabs play leads,
With wigs of seaweed for leafy steeds.
Each wave that crashes brings fame anew,
Like a soap opera, always in view.

The tide rolls in, fashion trends shift,
Conch shells become the latest gift.
There's a cast of mollusks with laughter clear,
Transforming the beach into a fun frontier.

So gather the shells, put on a show,
Where comedy reigns, and silliness flows.
In this salty world, we make our mark,
In tides of fun, we'll ignite the spark.

Submerged Thoughts

What lurks below in the ocean blue?
A fish that tells jokes, just for you.
With scales that shimmer like a bright disco,
His underwater giggle steals the show.

The seabed's cozy with tales untold,
Where clams gossip and secrets unfold.
"Did you hear the one about the seal?"
Crab snickers and shrieks, 'Oh, that's unreal!'

Anemones wave as if to shame,
Wiggling their tendrils, oh, what a game!
With every bubble, laughter flows,
In darkened depths, pure joy glows.

So dive right down, don't be a bore,
Join the corals in their lively lore.
In the depths of the sea, where wonders shift,
Every thought is a giggle, a wondrous gift.

Secrets in the Seafoam

In the froth, sea creatures plot,
Dancing dolphins, quite a lot.
Crabs wear hats, oh what a sight,
Underwater parties, full of light.

Jellyfish serve snacks so fine,
Sardines sip on fizzy brine.
Seahorses twirl, a trendy crowd,
Laughing under waves, feeling proud.

Octopuses play cards, joker's hand,
Clams have gossip, oh so grand.
Whales sing songs of silly fate,
Keeping secrets, never late.

Mermaids wink, they know the game,
Crafting legends, sharing fame.
In the bubble, joy will rise,
Under the sea, a grand surprise.

Shadows in the Flow

Bubbles rise from fishy pranks,
Clownfish laugh in funky ranks.
Eels wear shades, so suave and slick,
Swimming by with quite the trick.

Turtles race on current streams,
Silly dances, chasing dreams.
Starfish giggle, play the fool,
Making waves, it's such a rule.

Under the surface, shadows glide,
Creatures skedaddle, try to hide.
With every splash, laughter grows,
Flowing freely where the fun flows.

Anemones wave, laughing too,
"Best friends forever," they construe.
In the water's endless show,
Silly antics steal the flow.

Murmurs from the Abyss

Deep down where the darkness lies,
Funny fish share wild goodbyes.
A squid tells jokes, ink spills with glee,
While rays glide by, feeling so free.

"Why did the crab cross the floor?"
"Because it saw the ocean's door!"
Giggling shimmers from below,
Mysteries in the undertow.

Anglerfish with their glowing light,
Seek out laughs in the depths of night.
With each murmur, jokes take flight,
Silly tales in eternal night.

The depth may seem a little grim,
But here, each laugh grows ever dim.
In shadows thick, they find their cheer,
Murmuring jokes that all can hear.

The Undercurrent's Lament

In currents strong, the seaweed sways,
Fish enjoy the laughter's rays.
Bubbles pop with silly sounds,
As creatures frolic all around.

Starfish slide like slide on ice,
Slippery moves, oh so nice.
Shells chatter gossip, oh so bold,
Under the surface, stories told.

Tides pull jokes from every side,
No one knows where the jokes reside.
Whales and shrimp, a comedy act,
Making waves of laughter, that's a fact.

With every swell, they giggle bright,
In watery chambers, pure delight.
While laughter bounces with a twang,
The undercurrent hums its sang.

The Flow of Yesterday

Seagulls laugh as they dive and swoop,
While I trip over my own silly loop.
The waves tease my toes, oh how they play,
Making me question the skills of my sway.

Each splash is a giggle, a joke from the sea,
Tickling my ankles, so wild and free.
Casts of the nets filled with fish that bite,
But it's my luck that seems lost in the night.

Submerged Reflections

A mirror of bubbles and frilly seaweed,
Where fish make faces, oh what a deed!
I try to stare back, but they just swim on,
Perhaps they're laughing at my soggy con.

Floating along in this goofy parade,
I catch a starfish trying to serenade.
With each little swirl, the ocean is wry,
Sharing my secrets with a wink and a sigh.

The Depths of Distant Shores

At the beach, my ball has taken a dive,
In a race with a crab, oh what a vibe!
Salty slicks and slippery slides,
As I chase the giggles, my whole world glides.

Tidal tickles and marshmallow foam,
The shore keeps whispering, 'You're far from home!'
But laughter's the treasure, so rich and bright,
As I tumble and roll in the soft moonlight.

Currents of Unseen Emotion

In the ocean of feelings, I peek and I pry,
Where fish wear hats, and dolphins fly high.
Tides bring whispers from the depths so deep,
With humor afloat, how can I not leap?

Chasing my shadow, I meet a lost shoe,
It chuckles and says, 'You can't catch me too!'
With laughter that echoes from sun above,
Even the waves share their kindest love.

The Hidden Flow

In a world where secrets swim,
Fish gossip under the rim.
They whisper tales of silly pranks,
And plot their stealthy swanky flanks.

Octopuses juggling without a care,
While seahorses gossip, unaware.
Turtles in shades and fins so sleek,
Laughing at the dolphin's mystique.

Clownfish dancing in the swirl,
Making their own water pearl.
Every wave has a goofy twist,
In this ocean, humor can't be missed.

Where bubbles pop like jokes at plays,
And every foam finds clever ways.
Deep below, the chuckles rise,
In the depths, laughter underlies.

Depths of Silent Longing

A crab with dreams of sinking low,
Wants to tango with a baby chub, you know?
He practices steps with seaweed tight,
While starfish shrug, 'That's not quite right!'

Squid scribbling love notes in ink,
To fishy gal pals, they seldom think.
Their hearts float on waves of salty brine,
Yet octopus hides—he's drawing a line.

Shellfish sigh in a conch, so deep,
Watched by clams, as they giggle and peep.
If only the tides could set them free,
Or teach a lesson in harmony!

But here's the plot twist in the tale,
Mermaids forget they can't set sail.
Swaying gently, they sing lullabies,
Just to make seaweed feel like prize.

Strands of Lost Perspectives

Fish with glasses swim all askew,
In search of frames that come in blue.
They squint at the coral, worn and gray,
And wonder if the world's in disarray.

A shell's a phone that everyone dials,
But only crabs pick up with their smiles.
They giggle at swivel-headed glares,
While clownfish swim in mismatched pairs.

The moody rock, it just won't budge,
Rolling eyes in ocean sludge.
Conch shells tell tales of wild routine,
While sea cucumbers dance, looking serene.

Though underwater views can feel askew,
Laughter bubbles up, all fresh and new.
In the depths, what's lost is not so grim,
Just a wacky scene, and we all should swim!

Beneath the Surface

With a wink and a splash, the puffer laughs,
Blowing bubbles like quirky crafts.
A flounder tries to look so wise,
But fumbles, much to the angler's surprise.

Whales hum tunes in a goofy scale,
While jellyfish float like a dazzling veil.
They wink and sway in a synchronized jam,
And laugh as the sea turtles join in the bam!

Anemones wiggle, they think they're cool,
Getting lost in a conga line pool.
Fish shout, 'Dive!' while the seashells clash,
And rock the party with a bubbling splash.

Every wave hides a vibrant smile,
As creatures frolic in their own style.
Beneath the currents, a comedy show,
In the ocean's theatre, laughter flows!

The Language of the Sea

Seagulls squawk in fishy tones,
A clam replies with silent groans.
Starfish tell tales of lost socks,
While jellyfish play hopscotch on rocks.

The otters dance, slipping and sliding,
All while the crabs are sideways gliding.
Underwater there's a raucous cheer,
As whales serenade their fishy peers.

The barnacles gossip on hulls of old,
Sharing secrets in waters bold.
Octopuses juggle their hidden treasure,
With squids adding comedic measure.

The waves chuckle with each gentle roll,
As fish prank each other, that's their goal.
Seashells laugh with every new tide,
In this watery world, the fun won't hide.

Waves in the Stillness

The sea is calm, or so it seems,
But underneath, it bubbles with dreams.
Fishes plotting a wild parade,
While seaweed wands perform a charade.

The crabs are crafting their own ballet,
Twisting and turning in a merry sway.
A dolphin giggles, leaps in delight,
Adding humor with every height.

"Gotcha!" the octopus throws a prank,
Drapes himself as a seaweed bank.
The turtles roll their eyes in jest,
In this calm chaos, they know they're blessed.

When the sun dips low, and shadows blend,
The sea life knows how to transcend.
In the stillness, laughter extends,
A splash of joy among aquatic friends.

Reflections of the Deep

In the deep, the fish wear crowns,
Bobbing gently in jellyfish gowns.
They giggle as bubbles start to rise,
Swapping tales 'neath the salty skies.

Anemones wave in flowing grace,
Sea cucumbers join the race.
With barnacle blinks and winked regards,
They throw a ball made of sea shards.

"Who can spin faster?" a clam does shout,
As crustaceans cheer and spin about.
A seahorse judges with a conch-shell clap,
While the sea snails crawl in a turtled nap.

Then a whale makes a splash, what a mess!
Sending fish flying in joyous distress.
In the deep, it's a laugh riot, indeed,
Flipping finned foes in a comedy breed.

Echoes in the Mist

Misty mornings bring echoes clear,
As fish trade jokes that only they hear.
The tide whispers secrets soft and low,
While the sea critters steal the show.

A crab tells a tale with a sideways glance,
About a jellyfish caught in a trance.
The dolphin rolls, capturing the light,
Making misty morning mean pure delight.

Eels slither through with a wobbly wiggle,
Tickling fish that just want to giggle.
Barnacles chuckle with each wave's kiss,
In the salty air, they laugh at bliss.

As fog drifts in and the sun starts to rise,
The sea holds wonders, a great surprise.
Each splashing sound and whispering breeze,
Is a comic joy, carried with ease.

Tides of Time and Memory

The clock strikes funny, oh what a sight,
A fish in a bowtie thinks he's quite bright.
Dancing with seaweed, oh what a joke,
While hermit crabs giggle, beneath the ocean smoke.

Each wave's a hiccup, moon's in a suit,
Starfish are laughing, they've got no dispute.
Coconuts floating, helmets on heads,
As seagulls make puns over sandy beds.

Sandcastles wobble, like jelly up high,
Seashells are snickering, as they wave goodbye.
The tide pulls back, but laughs linger near,
In an underwater comedy, we shed a tear.

Yet memories bubble, in salty delight,
Every chuckle echoes, through day and night.
With laughter on currents, we drift without fear,
In the ocean of moments, we savor each cheer.

Shadows on the Shore

Footprints in sand, a shadowly dance,
Crabs throwing parties, they take their chance.
With a wave and a wink, the tide rolls in,
While gulls tell tall tales, with a mischievous grin.

A turtle in shades, he's stealing the scene,
While dolphins provide the comical sheen.
Sunbathers yell, 'Hey! Watch out for that!'
But the shadows just giggle, in a beachy spat.

As the sun dips low, with a cheeky flair,
The shadows stretch long, making shapes in the air.
The tide giggles back, with a tickle and swish,
Life's a sandy joke, with every splash and swish.

And when the moon rises, it winks at the sand,
While shadows mix puns, like a cabaret band.
The beach holds its secrets, but tonight it's all right,
With laughter and whispers, beneath the starlight.

Murmurs of the Deep

In the depths of the sea, bubbles start to burst,
Funny fish fortunes, flip over first.
A clam claims his crown, in a regal pose,
While octopuses dance, with eight-legged prose.

Whispers of laughter, in currents that spin,
With the sun shining down, the merriment's in.
Starfish tell stories, with a twinkle of light,
While everyone chuckles, at the playful sight.

The sharks throw a party, with snacks made of cheese,
While turtles toast shells, 'To the deep! Now, please!'
The jellyfish jiggle, with a glow in the dark,
Creating a spectacle, like sparks in a park.

In the blue, there's a jest, an underwater dream,
Where every wave giggles, and bubbles can scream.
With murmurs of joy, let's dance to the sound,
In the depths of our laughter, true happiness found.

Undercurrents of the Heart

In the depths of my chest, beats a chuckling wave,
A rhythm of joy, oh how it behaves.
Fish tickle my pinky, and flip-flop around,
While the tide whispers secrets, joyfully profound.

With conch shells for laughter, they echo the glee,
As sea creatures plot, a big comedy spree.
A squid writes a script, with ink on the go,
While dolphins play lead, putting on quite a show.

While fed by the heart, the deep plays its part,
Making moods lighter, a flowing work of art.
The laughter that bubbles, fuels the calm sea,
In the undercurrents, find humor in me.

Within this vast ocean, a heart learns to play,
With growing designs, a colorful array.
In the laughter of waves, we'll dance 'til we part,
Because life's an adventure, from the depths of the heart.

Embracing the Unseen

In the ocean, fish wear smiles,
Their fins are flapping with such styles.
A crab's dancing like it's on a spree,
While seagulls shout, "Hey, look at me!"

The jellyfish aimlessly float around,
While seaweed tickles, no one's found.
A dolphin sneezes, the bubble bursts,
And laughter spreads, with fins it first.

Under the waves, where secrets creep,
The octopus holds a funny peek.
"Heck, why hide, when we can tease?"
With hidden giggles, they float with ease.

In the depths where no one seeks,
The sea cucumbers boast with squeaks.
Frolicking fins, such a radical sight,
In the depth's embrace, everything's light.

The Lure of Indecision

A starfish wonders where to roam,
Should it stay or go back home?
It flipped a coin with such great flair,
But it just ended up nowhere.

The clownfish can't decide a role,
Is it a jester or in control?
It dances left, then twirls to right,
Confused by laughter in day and night.

A sea turtle stops, oh what a tease,
"Should I nap or swim with ease?"
It checks the clock made out of coral,
Still unsure, it starts to twirl.

Indecision swirls with each tide,
The ocean chuckles, how can it hide?
Between the laughs and playful looks,
The choices sparkle like favorite books.

Silent Movements

Anemones sway without a sound,
While goofy fish dart all around.
They play peek-a-boo in their little homes,
Making bubbles, talking in tones.

A shy shrimp blushes in the sand,
Almost giggling at a crab's funny stand.
The hermit crab wears shells too bright,
In a swap meet adventure, such delight!

The seahorse winks, takes a bow,
"I'm the star, the sea says wow!"
Silent dances become a spree,
In a world that's wild and endlessly free.

Whispers of laughter weave the tide,
While fish flip-flop with glee and pride.
In the silence of the ocean's grace,
Comes the joy of a playful race.

Resounding Currents

The waves all laugh with a booming cheer,
As crabs play jokes, they hint and sneer.
A fishy prince loses his crown,
As currents swirl and spin him around.

With bubbles rising, a sea horse jokes,
"Do you hear the sound of our funny hopes?"
The ocean roars with gurgles and fun,
As starfish join in and dance as one.

The sea otter spins in a woven dance,
Catching seaweed as if by chance.
"Let's ride these currents, come join the ride!"
With laughter echoing, they glide with pride.

Resounding waves bring mirth to the deep,
Where every creature has joy to reap.
So let's dive down beneath the glee,
And dance in seas of hilarity!

Waves of Subtle Undertones

In the ocean's sway, fish swim with flair,
Juggling seaweed without a care,
A crab in a tux, looking quite spry,
Dances on shells as the waves roll by.

Seagulls steal fries, with a squawk and a dive,
Their antics enough to keep dreams alive,
While clams play poker on a sandy table,
Offering laughter, if we're willing and able.

Jellyfish float like balloons on a spree,
Waving hello, as if to say, "Me!"
The ocean's a circus, a watery show,
With laughter and giggles, a bubbly flow.

So come take a dip, don't be shy, my friend,
In this comical sea where the giggles send,
Each wave brings a joke, each splash a delight,
In the sunny playground of day and night.

Echoes in the Deep

Underwater echoes spill out in glee,
As fish share their secrets, oh so carefree,
A whale's hearty laugh shakes the sea floor,
Sending bubbles that quirkily soar.

Octopus in shades sits sipping his drink,
Picking up seashells, he gives them a wink,
"Why did the coral never get a job?"
"It couldn't get past the reef's snobby mob!"

Starfish play cards, each one with a grin,
As sea turtles roll their eyes at the din,
A clam tells the best jokes, but no one can hear,
Just a dull thud when he covers his ear.

The deeps are a party, festooned with jest,
Where the fishfolk convene, it's simply the best,
So dive on in, don't let fun pass you by,
In this depths of laughter, always make time to try!

Currents of Unseen Whispers

A school of fish chats with playful grace,
Trading tall tales of a mermaid's face,
"Oh please, not again!" they giggle and swirl,
As a dolphin leaps, doing a flip and a twirl.

The sea floor's a stage; a crab's doing hip hop,
He moonwalks on sand, then performs a big flop,
"Seems I'm not cut out for the dance of the tide,
But I'll stick with my jokes; there's fun here to ride!"

Clownfish get lost, in anemone's hug,
Deciding that's home, they give it a shrug,
While sonar warnings echo through waves,
"Lost fish at sea? What's wrong with their braves?"

With laughter and joy at the current's command,
The ocean's a place, where giggles expand,
So travel these waters and you shall discover,
That humor's the treasure, like no other.

The Dance of Hidden Depths

In the murky blue, a treasure chest grins,
While a fish tries to hide, but its giggle gives in,
"Why are treasures so up to their tricks?"
"Because they just love to give golds and quick flicks!"

The starfish all waltz, albeit a bit slow,
In sync with the tides, they put on a show,
They tap dance on rocks, making shells rattle,
While otters and seals cheer from their battle.

Bubbles escape with a ticklish sigh,
"Did you hear that? A fish took a pie!"
The seaweed laughs, gets tangled in fun,
As the joy of the ocean shines bright like the sun.

So swim down below, in this comedic spree,
Where laughter flows freely, as deep as can be,
And join in the dance, let your spirits rise high,
For in the deep blue, there's humor nearby!

Subtle Changes

A fish swims by, with a wink so sly,
It twirls and swirls, as bubbles fly.
The seaweed giggles in a dance so bold,
While crabs wear hats, quite warm and old.

The starfish sighs, saying, 'What a tease!'
As jellyfish float with such perfect ease.
A splash of joy in every splashy dive,
Who knew the ocean could be so alive?

A hermit crab makes a home from a shoe,
Says, 'I'll take this look—it's chic and new!'
Seagulls are sneaking a sandwich or two,
While fish trade gossip about the view!

The tide goes out, and the beach has a laugh,
As sandcastles tumble, they dance in half.
But worry not, the waves come to play,
Making sure the fun never fades away.

The Heart's Underbelly

Beneath the waves, where the lights twinkle bright,
The octopus stirs, oh what a sight!
With eight little arms, it juggles a pearl,
'Watch out!' yells the clam, 'You'll give me a whirl!'

A lobster in slippers walks down the lane,
Says, 'Oh dear, it's my fashion campaign!'
With a pinch and a pose, it smiles with glee,
While fish take selfies, how funny to see!

The sea cucumber's feeling quite flat,
Wishing for scales or a tail—imagine that!
As shrimp play poker, they giggle and grin,
'Who knew a card game could lead to a win?'

A whale in a tutu gives a grand twirl,
As dolphins applaud with a joyful whirl.
In quirky ballet, they dance side by side,
Beneath the waves, where chaos and fun collide!

Beyond the Visible

In depths unseen, where shadows wiggle,
A mystery lurks, giving quite a giggle.
'There's a fish with legs!' says a curious trout,
'No way,' sighs a crab, 'You must be out!'

They tell silly tales of a mermaid's grin,
Whose laugh sounds like bubbles—where to begin?
With tales of treasure that's nothing but junk,
The parrotfish rolls its eyes with a hunk!

A sea urchin claims it's an ancient sage,
Writing grand novels as it turns the page.
But all it scribbles is 'Ouch!' and 'Gee!'
As the ocean chuckles, 'That's not so witty!'

Each creature a character in jest and cheer,
With underwater jokes—let's give a cheer!
For in this blue world, where secrets are spun,
We find the laughter—splashing, splashy fun!

Convergences Below

Where currents twist in whimsical ways,
Creatures collide, sharing their plays.
A dolphin does cartwheels with grace and flair,
While a flatfish stares with a questioning glare.

Turtles chat gossip, passing the tide,
'Have you seen the crab in a daring slide?'
Amid coral castles, the fish laugh and tease,
As a squid interrupts, shouting, 'Look at me, please!'

Manta rays glide in their elegant sweep,
While the sea cucumber tries not to sleep.
Glowing sea anemones catch the sight,
Telling tales of starry, magical night!

Beneath waves of wonder, friendships ignite,
In this silly world, where all is just right.
From the tiny to great, with a bubble and squish,
The ocean's a circus—a comedic wish!

Dreams of the Deep Blue

In the ocean's dance, fish wear hats,
While octopuses juggle with shiny sprats.
Turtles play poker on coral reefs,
And crabs tell jokes that bring forth laughs.

Seahorses race on seaweed tracks,
Anemones cheer with soft, flowing backs.
Clams hide pearl secrets, grin with pride,
All while the current offers a ride.

Dolphins do somersaults, show off their flair,
As wiggly worms dance without a care.
The jellyfish rave in the shimmering light,
What a sight, what a sight, in the depth of the night!

So dive in and join this peculiar spree,
Where the ocean's antics are wild and free.
With every splash, there's a tale to tell,
In this crazy realm, all creatures dwell.

The Edges of Reflection

At the surface, bubbles float and pop,
While starfish judge from their rocky top.
A fish in sunglasses poses for style,
Offering grins that stretch a mile.

The sea turtles gossip about beach trends,
While plankton dance in their tiny blends.
A gnome in the sand waves a tiny flag,
As crabs scuttle by with a merry brag.

The seagulls giggle with beaks wide and grinning,
Sharing tales of their latest skimming.
Mollusks boast of their shimmering shells,
Painting the stories of oceanic spells.

So look down below, where the fun never ends,
Nature's humor is rich, it always sends.
With every flick of a tail, they find joy,
In the watery world, life's the real McCoy!

Underwater Whispers

In the deep, where the whispers swim,
Eels play tag on a light-hearted whim.
Crabs gossip about the best hiding spots,
While plankton enjoy gossiping plots.

Turtles narrate tales of their long, wild chases,
And fishes wear crowns in glimmering phases.
Octopuses stretch for a game of charades,
As the ocean applauds with its gentle cascades.

A mermaid sings songs that tickle the reef,
Adding laughter beneath, like a comic relief.
Whale songs rumble, bringing chuckles galore,
As the sea calls for fun on its vibrant floor.

So dip into laughter, let worry subside,
Embrace the ocean's joy, let it be your guide.
For beneath the surface, where laughter awakes,
The underwater world is filled with fun, no fakes!

The Lattice of Hidden Life

In the lattice of life, where the sea whispers soft,
A clownfish tells jokes, giving everyone a scoff.
Anemones giggle, tickled to their core,
As sea cucumbers crawl with tales to explore.

Barnacles bust out in a one-man show,
While gobies flit by in a synchronized flow.
Lobsters wear sunglasses, strutting with pride,
In this hidden kingdom, where laughter won't hide.

So let's take a dive into this bustling space,
Where each creature's antics bring a smiling face.
For humor swims deep where the seaweed sways,
In the lattice of life, we frolic for days!

Beneath the Foam

The fish threw a party, oh what a sight,
With bubbles and giggles, they danced through the night.
A crab on a fiddle, a clam with a drum,
They jiggled and wiggled, oh how they did strum.

A seaweed confetti rained down from above,
The jellyfish boogied, in rhythm with love.
They splashed and they clashed, such a comical crew,
While the dolphin just laughed, saying, "What's wrong with you?"

An octopus chef flipped some fishy delight,
But someone yelled, "Caution! That's not quite a bite!"
With tentacles tangled, they managed a feast,
Leaving all kinds of chaos—at least they had yeast!

So if you're ocean-bound and feel quite the bore,
Just dive in the fun—there's plenty in store!
A splash here, a splash there, just let out a cheer,
Beneath the foam's laughter, there's nothing to fear!

The Echo of Unseen Waves

In underwater realms where secrets collide,
A clam told a tale of a snail that could glide.
"Are you sure it's true?" asked a bright little trout,
"I'm still picking up seaweed; what's that about?"

The shrimp with a wink piped in with a grin,
"Why float when you can do the twist with a spin?"
They all took a turn, in a dance full of glee,
As the bubbles erupted, like popcorn from sea!

A sea cucumber jumped but forgot how to land,
Crashing right down, it looked quite unplanned.
"Did you see that flop?" shouted a sardine in jest,
"Next time aim for grace, not that flailing quest!"

Yet laughter resounded through each nook and each cranny,
For in this odd world, everything's quite zany.
In the echo of bubbles, the giggles entwine,
A legacy of joy as the fish all align.

Chords of the Deep

A whale played a tune with a splash and a swish,
"Hey, listen up, folks! I've a grand new dish!"
The clownfish all chuckled, they snorted with cheer,
As the sea star tapped toes to the beat loud and clear.

The angelfish fluttered, doing flips in the swell,
While the sea horse strummed on a clamshell carousel.
Crabs clapped their claws, keeping rhythm with zest,
"More funk, less flunk!"—it was quite an odd fest!

With each note they played, the ocean would sway,
As an eel played the bass in a jazzy display.
"Just keep it down, buddy! I've a date with this sand!"
The sand dollar winked, "Just give me a hand!"

So they jammed on through twilight, a gig full of fun,
The tides rolled around as the music was spun.
In the depths of the sea, the chorus ran deep,
With chords that made everyone dance from their sleep!

The Veil of Water

Behind the bright waves, a mystery's brewing,
A sponge just declared, "I've been never renewing!"
The clownfish thought twice, then burst into song,
"It's fine to stay home; we've been busy too long!"

Amongst the kelp forest, a party was set,
Where starfish threw snacks, such a culinary bet.
"A touch of sea salt, a twist and a flip,
Does anyone want to join us for a dip?"

With giggles and splashes, they feasted with glee,
The sea cucumbers brought a sponge cake for free.
The turtles just smiled, they knew their grand plan,
To win over hearts with the snacks of their clan!

So down in the depths, with laughter galore,
Every sea creature danced like never before.
Behind bubbles and laughter, a world full of cheer,
In the veil of the water, there's joy to draw near!

www.ingramcontent.com/pod-product-compliance
Lightning Source LLC
Chambersburg PA
CBHW060145230426
43661CB00003B/580